Write Your Way To Success

Lessons Learned on my Path from Ordinary Developer to Author of Programming Books That Sell

Azat Mardan

Apress®

Write Your Way To Success

Azat Mardan
San Francisco, CA, USA

ISBN-13 (pbk): 978-1-4842-3969-8   ISBN-13 (electronic): 978-1-4842-3970-4
https://doi.org/10.1007/978-1-4842-3970-4

Library of Congress Control Number: 2018963599

Managing Director, Apress Media LLC: Welmoed Spahr
Acquisitions Editor: Louise Corrigan
Development Editor: James Markham
Coordinating Editor: Nancy Chen

Cover designed by eStudioCalamar
Cover image designed by Freepik (www.freepik.com)

Distributed to the book trade worldwide by Springer Science+Business Media New York, 233 Spring Street, 6th Floor, New York, NY 10013. Phone 1-800-SPRINGER, fax (201) 348-4505, e-mail orders-ny@springer-sbm.com, or visit www.springeronline.com. Apress Media, LLC is a California LLC and the sole member (owner) is Springer Science + Business Media Finance Inc (SSBM Finance Inc). SSBM Finance Inc is a **Delaware** corporation.

For information on translations, please e-mail rights@apress.com, or visit http://www.apress.com/rights-permissions.

Apress titles may be purchased in bulk for academic, corporate, or promotional use. eBook versions and licenses are also available for most titles. For more information, reference our Print and eBook Bulk Sales web page at http://www.apress.com/bulk-sales.

Any source code or other supplementary material referenced by the author in this book is available to readers on GitHub via the book's product page, located at www.apress.com/9781484239698. For more detailed information, please visit http://www.apress.com/source-code.

Printed on acid-free paper

Table of Contents

TABLE OF CONTENTS

About the Author

Azat Mardan is a software engineering leader at Indeed.com, and a JavaScript/Node.js expert with several online courses on Udemy and Node University, and 18 books published on the topic, including top-sellers *React Quickly* (Manning, 2016), *Full Stack JavaScript* (Apress, 2015), *Practical Node.js* (Apress, 2014), and *Pro Express.js* (Apress, 2014).

In his spare time, Azat writes about tech on Webapplog.com, speaks at conferences, and contributes to open source. Before becoming an expert in Node.js, Azat finished his Master's in Information Systems Technology and worked at US federal government agencies, small startups, and big corporations with various technologies, including Java, SQL, PHP, and Ruby.

Azat is passionate about technology and finance, as well as new ways of educating and empowering people.

Foreword

"Developers don't pay for things."

That was the resounding message I heard when I told people I was working on a book to help programmers get better at designing iOS apps. I'm glad I didn't listen.

Two years ago I started down a path that took me from being an unknown freelance designer to making more than $500,000 from self-published books. Those who say developers don't pay for things—especially books—couldn't be more wrong.

You see, as a programmer you are in a unique position: you know a valuable skill. More people are learning to code than ever before. Demand for developers is high and developer salaries are reaching incredible levels—meaning coding is a skill that makes money.

When you teach a skill that makes money, readers who understand the concept of a return on investment will make a simple value judgment and buy with confidence because they know the new skill will be worth far more than the cost of a book.

Spending $39 on a book is nothing if it means a $5,000 raise that year or the potential to get a new job that could pay $10,000 more! Developers who want to advance their careers are happy to pay for training that will help them.

You have the skills; now it's time to start teaching. You don't have to wait for permission from a publisher—after all, self-publishing is the most profitable way to go—or wait to have an audience.

Start writing your book and building your audience at the same time. If you keep at it you'll have a healthy side income from your own book very soon.

I'll let Azat take it from here and show you exactly how it's done.

—Nathan Barry[1]

Author of *The App Design Handbook*[2],

Designing Web Applications[3],

and *Authority*[4]

---

[1]http://nathanbarry.com/

[2]http://nathanbarry.com/app-design-handbook

[3]http://nathanbarry.com/webapps

[4]http://nathanbarry.com/authority

Introduction

Write Your Way To Success is my story of the lessons that I've learned on my journey from ordinary software engineer / developer to successful writer, who has published six expert books (and counting). Two of them stayed on the Amazon #1 Best Seller List in the Client-Server category for a few weeks—and I've secured two traditional publishing deals. Now, my books generate enough passive income that I could quit my day job, pick only interesting projects to work on, and focus on what's important to me.

This phenomenon is not unique to me or Node.js. There are multiple examples of authors[1] making anywhere from $10,000 to $130,000 per book. Nathan Barry[2], Sacha Greif[3], Reg Braithwaite[4], and Josh Earl[5] are among them. If they did it, and I did it, you can too, and you don't have to be a master like Hemingway or Nabokov.

Who This Book Is For

This book is aimed at intermediate and advanced

- Software engineers

- Designers

- Front-end developers

- Mobile developers

In general, this book is for any experts (or wannabe experts) in technical topics, tools, frameworks for web development, applied computer science (i.e., practical fields), dev ops, and QA.

What This Book Is

Write Your Way To Success is my personal story mainly aimed at encouraging new technical authors to start writing. It shows my mistakes and achievements to illustrate how easy self-publishing has become. And this trend will only continue.

---

[1]https://leanpub.com/amillionlessons
[2]http://nathanbarry.com/2013-review
[3]https://nathanbarry.com/nathan-barry-sacha-greif-sold-39k-worth-ebooks/
[4]http://blog.leanpub.com/2012/05/reg-braithwaite.html
[5]http://blog.leanpub.com/2014/01/leanpub-ebook-sales-guest-post.html

Then, I give some practical tips about publishing and marketing. Last but not least, the appendixes provide some useful information such as lists of tools. So there are four distinct parts:

- *Story*: My two-year journey into writing books
- *ProgWriter*: About the process
- *Publishing*: How to publish
- *Marketing*: How to market

What This Book Is Not

This book is not a step-by-step guide on how to self-publish your book with a particular platform or tool, because they all evolve so fast, and to keep up with all the new services would require a weekly update. They die and become obsolete fast as well.

Of course there's more than one way to skin a cat. Authors achieve success by building platforms and then marketing books to them. Or, vice versa, they gain a following by publishing books. This title is my personal interpretation of techniques, events, and trends, so take it with a grain of salt.

How to Use the Book

This book is best when read in one sitting, preferably somewhere nice and accompanied by a delightful caffeinated beverage. Please make notes and highlight as you go along to improve effectiveness of retention.

At the beginning of each chapter are helpful summaries that encapsulate in a few short sentences what examples and topics that particular chapter covers.

Terms

For the purpose of this book, we'll use some terms interchangeably, although, depending on the context, they might not mean exactly the same thing. For example:

- framework = library = module

- software engineer = developer = programmer

- application = program = script

Now we are done with introductions, let's jump straight to how I did what I did, that is my story.

CHAPTER 1

My Story

To get things started, I'll tell how I started in software engineering and ended up as a writer of programming books.

Humble Beginnings

I think I've always had an itch for creating products using virtual means, and a love for bits produced by keystrokes and the electric power in computers. The bits turn into pixels on the screen, which turn into

© Azat Mardan 2019
A. Mardan, *Write Your Way To Success*, https://doi.org/10.1007/978-1-4842-3970-4_1

something beautiful and useful to others. Writing code and writing books are very similar activities in this sense. In both cases, we begin with a blank file and slowly fill it with characters. The manuscript and code are usually poorly written at first and later morph into something stunning (at least we'd like to think so... until editors and quality assurance [QA] make a pass) such as the app or a book.

My first serious publications were internal university workshop textbooks released in 2002. They were about 40-60 pages long and contained a lot of code, and I proudly showed my name to anybody I knew. The funny thing is that the next year, my classmates at the university had to use my manuals to do the workshops, and they didn't like them at all. The text underwent a few revisions before printing—so I learned my lesson: it's important to have creative control. And self-publishing is great for that.

After graduating from the Bachelor's program, I did consulting for various US government agencies. Due to the way they work, developers regularly moved from one project to another. Each project was built on a different stack and lasted anywhere from three to twelve months. That gave me a chance to work with many languages and platforms: Java, PHP, ASP, VB, SQL, XML, and more. You name it—I used it. I had to develop a generalist mentality and sharp learning skills to get up to speed quickly. Most of the projects had no, zero, zip, nada documentation. This taught me that *the best documentation is the source code.*

I liked the illusionary security of federally funded projects, but I wanted to grow in my profession. For this reason, I joined a startup that was accepted to the prestigious 500 Startups business accelerator in Mountain View, California. And this is how I ended up in the Bay Area, where I live now.

I didn't go back to writing books until I moved to Silicon Valley and taught myself Ruby on Rails in a week. It wasn't expert level, of course, but enough to start building my own apps, instead of following the book[1].

---

[1]http://pragprog.com/book/rails4/agile-web-development-with-rails-4

I loved Rails because it did so many things for me. But I felt like it was already quite mature, and had (and still has) a large following. And if I was going to learn and get better at something new to me, why not bet on something more up-and-coming like Node.js? Especially because I always used JavaScript, and the language itself is not as weird to me as Ruby (with its fat arrows => and colons).

These reasons, and the fact that I failed five or six RoR interviews in 2012—everyone was looking for more senior Ruby developers—led me on my journey to learn Node.js.

Learning Node.js

Up until that point, I'd spent my entire career writing code, and I was pretty *ordinary* at that. Things started to shift when I decided to document my Node.js baby steps so that I could refer to them later. The added benefit of doing that was that I could share the notes with other developers on my blog.

Then I remembered that *the best learning is when you teach somebody else*. With this in mind, I approached the StartupMonthly[2] venture firm and startup incubator with an idea of an immersive JavaScript and Node.js training course, which we called *Rapid Prototyping with JS* (Figure 1-1), because initially, it was aimed at startupers.

---

[2]http://startupmonthly.org

Figure 1-1. *Rapid Prototyping with JS training*

Then, I published the notes, posts, and the manual from the training using Leanpub, which became the *Rapid Prototyping with JS: Agile JavaScript Development* book.

In the meantime, I wrote a few apps, like HackHall.com[3], and was hired by the Node.js pioneer and Joyent[4] partner, a startup called Storify[5]. What attracted me to Storify was the fact that its whole stack—and not just some part of it—was run on Node.js! In a small team of five engineers I quickly[6] leveled up in Node.js while continuing to blog tutorials and churn out side projects like MongoUI[7].

Soon after that, I had enough work experience and blogging experience to start teaching others at Hack Reactor[8], Marakana[9] (split into

---

[3]http://hackhall.com

[4]http://joyent.com

[5]http://storify.com

[6]http://webapplog.com/first-six-months-with-storify

[7]www.npmjs.org/package/mongoui

[8]http://hackreactor.com

[9]http://marakana.com

Twitter University and ProTech[10] after the acquisition by Twitter), General Assembly[11], and PARISOMA[12].

After publishing and selling a few hundred copies of *Rapid Prototyping with JS*, I got some feedback and I wanted to write a better book. In the meantime, my blog traffic grew from a meager 20 visitors to 400-600 visitors per day in 2013. I've noticed that one of my blog posts gets 15-25% of my total traffic. The post[13] was about the Express.js framework. Given that interest, I decided to focus on the trendy Express.js topic. A friend of mine who worked as the technical editor said that the best books are the ones that focus on one topic and dominate it. So the concept of the *Express.js Guide* as a comprehensive manual was born.

Mastering a Niche

I tried to incorporate all the lessons I learned from *Rapid Prototyping with JS* into *Express.js Guide*. I wrote four apps as examples and provided an extensive overview of the framework's application programming interface (API) by reading its source code and lackluster documentation.

I set a deadline for myself and created a Gumroad page. The example set by Nathan Barry's books immediately convinced me to try Gumroad in addition to Leanpub. For more info on storefronts, check out Chapter 5.

After that, I wrote a few blog posts and made announcements about *Express.js Guide*. I started using ads for my own books—I had two more smaller-sized books in addition to *Rapid Prototyping with JS* and *Express.js Guide*—on my blog more extensively. Consequently, the effort resulted in

---

[10]http://thenewcircle.com
[11]http://generalassemb.ly
[12]http://parisoma.com
[13]http://bit.ly/2jfAztk

about 150 pre-order sales at a discounted price of $10. Not bad money for one day at all!

After the *Express.js Guide* launch (which coincided with me joining DocuSign[14]), the traffic from my blog and the book's web site helped sales. These web properties were often on the first page search results on Google. But the real game changer in terms of the revenue happened when I put *Rapid Prototyping with JS* and *Express.js Guide* on Amazon via Kindle Direct Publishing. Amazon, just like Leanpub, attracts new customers because it is a huge marketplace, and my work attracted new interest, in addition to my regular blog readers. Also, I used bundles with prominent Leanpub best sellers to get additional exposure.

Now I knew that my books could become a serious passive income source. All I needed to do was to write 10 or, even better, 20 books like *Express.js Guide*.

In January 2014 I flew to the New Media Expo in Las Vegas, Nevada, where I learned *How to Sell Books by the Truckload on Amazon.com*[15] directly from the author of this book. That same night, I flew back, I tweaked my Amazon product pages (more on this in Chapter 5), and whoosh! *Express.js Guide* became an *Amazon #1 Best Seller* in the Client-Server category. The week after, *Rapid Prototyping with JS* followed suit and pushed *Express.js Guide* to #2 on the list. The conference session's tips made a difference, along with positive reviews from Hack Reactor students (to whom I gifted the book) and Leanpub readers.

---

[14]http://webapplog.com/good-bye-storify

[15]http://www.amazon.com/How-Sell-Books-Truckload-Amazon-com-ebook/dp/
    B00IOB92SS

Going Traditional

After thousands of downloads on Leanpub, Gumroad, and Amazon, I still wasn't completely happy. I felt like I could gain more readership and learn better writing and structuring by traditionally publishing a new book. I approached several publishers, and pitched *Express.js Guide* to them, but nothing materialized.

Another concept I had in mind was an all-in-one book that covers every important aspect of modern web development: database, OAuth, WebSocket, template engines, frameworks, and deployments. I picked up a book covering those topics but was disappointed. I can do better, I thought, so I wrote a new proposal, which was eventually accepted by a publisher. I started writing the Practical Node.js manuscript in October-November of 2013. I devoted my weekends and holidays to it (as so many entrepreneurs and writers do). The original publishing date was sometime in March. I had the manuscript ready by January-February. I think the work went relatively fast for a 300-page manuscript because:

- I used published blog posts and drafts of unpublished blog posts.

- I used code samples from my side projects like blog-express[16] and todo-express[17].

- I used Markdown, and only when I was done did I convert the files into MS Word using PanDoc (a wonderful tool).

- I used app examples from my declined Progmatic proposal.

---

[16]https://github.com/azat-co/blog-express
[17]https://github.com/azat-co/todo-express

To summarize, having blog posts and side-project apps allowed me to write the manuscript faster while still working two jobs (DocuSign[18] and Hack Reactor[19]).

I've shared more details about the *Practical Node.js* writing process in my blog post "Getting Published as a Programmer: The *Practical Node.js* Story."[20]

In the middle of editing the *Practical Node.js* book, Express.js version 4 came out. I convinced my editors to let me update the text and code samples.

Practical Node.js went to print in July 2014 and became the first book on Express.js v 4.x.

Somewhere along the almost two years since I'd published the first version of *Rapid Prototyping with JS*, I was approached by international publishers. In my opinion, they offer great deals, because without heavy lifting I can increase my readership and earn more in advances and royalties! They typically translate, publish (print and digital), and distribute my books. They also pay adequate advances and reasonable royalties. So far I've signed contracts with Chinese and Korean companies. Overall, I might have spent 30 to 60 minutes sending emails with contract, manuscript, and code files—the easiest money ever!

Each book I've completed is its own journey, and I've learned something through each new process.

The major technical publisher Apress is publishing the last two books on the list. You might ask, "Why be a programmer writer (progwriter)?" or "Why go the traditional publishing route?" Chapter 2 addresses these topics, so read on.

---

[18]http://docusign.com
[19]http://hackreactor.com
[20]http://bit.ly/2jh8kdF

CHAPTER 2

ProgWriter

So why write programming *books* when there are a lot of free online resources (portals, YouTube videos, slides, presentations, and podcasts) and other less competitive products like software itself? Or why write *programming* books and not vampire novels that have a bigger market?

In this chapter, I'll cover the following topics:

- Why write books?

- Why write a *programming* book?

- Traditional vs. self-publishing

© Azat Mardan 2019
A. Mardan, *Write Your Way To Success*, https://doi.org/10.1007/978-1-4842-3970-4_2

Why Write Books?

Why bother with writing books? Why can't we just keep writing software? I'm often asked about these questions, and each time, I'm reassured that writing about technology or techniques helps me in many ways in which pure coding can't because

- It provides a better and deeper understanding of a particular technology and is a means of explaining it to others (not just grasping concepts intuitively, which often happens when all that the programmers do is write code).

- It creates motivation to research, learn, and document some obscure functionalities, features, and pitfalls that otherwise likely would have never been discovered just by using the code. For example, some Express.js configurations probably would have taken me months and years of development to discover, because they are not necessary in day-to-day tasks, but knowing and using these configs can greatly enhance the quality of code and the product.

- Practicing better written communication is paramount to achieving success in our careers or businesses in our *asynchronous* world (e.g., documenting, communicating via e-mail, and writing marketing copy), because people text and e-mail instead of calling; and at work we write IMs, e-mails, and JIRA tickets instead of talking in person.

- Developing the skills to formalize ideas and thoughts is a must for technical leaders who need to learn, practice, and improve their ability to persuade (and their ability to present their ideas in the best way).

- Establishing yourself as a thought leader in technology
  will boost your job security, improve recruiting/hiring
  appeal (when you are hiring others), and help you
  get speaking engagements at conferences (e.g., my
  QConNY 2014[1] speech about CoffeeScript[2]), meetups,
  and trainings.

- It can create a source of passive income to supplement
  your fluctuating freelance income or even regular
  income.

- It can help others to avoid the frustration of making
  the mistakes that you've made, save them time, and
  enable them to learn new technologies faster and more
  effectively (time to market is faster for self-publishing
  and blogging).

- If you make a mistake in the code, the whole thing
  won't work, but if you make 10 or 20 typos in the book,
  it won't prevent readers from getting value. Hey, most
  readers won't even notice them!

ⓘ Info   A fun anecdotal behavior that I've noticed: *most people don't read books*, and programmers don't read books even more. Sometimes I receive reviews or comments from people who clearly didn't bother to read even the Introduction of the books. The article "Programmers Don't Read Books—But You Should"[3] supports my observation. On average, software engineers read zero books per

---

[1]https://qconnewyork.com
[2]http://infoq.com/presentations/coffeescript-lessons
[3]http://blog.codinghorror.com/programmers-dont-read-books-but-you-should

year. But they sure buy them. Some put them on shelves or use them as monitor stands[4] while others skim through the Table of Contents and borrow code examples that they can possibly use in their latest projects.

I want to caution you, though. *The path to writing programming books is not a get rich quick scheme.* There are no shortcuts, but if you approach it seriously, it can generate a fair income. As was mentioned before, I've met dozens of technical authors online and in person who've made anywhere from $10,000 to $130,000 on a single book, usually in a span of just a few months, by working on it part-time in addition to their full-time jobs or freelance projects.

The best part is that after a relatively intense and active period of writing and publishing, you can enjoy the income *passively*! This beats even Software as a Service (SaaS) products because they require ongoing support and maintenance. Aside from fixing bugs and typos once in a while in new releases, books are pretty much an upload and forget thing. In other words, you have the potential to make money without putting in hours of labor. You can make money in your sleep! It was fascinating to wake up in the morning and check my inbox: one, two, or three sales of *Rapid Prototyping with JS* via Leanpub. Whoo-hoo! The magic of passive recurring income is obvious. But I noticed that other aspects of the process were more important to me in the beginning when I had zero sales: improving my understanding (sometimes learning something from scratch) and my thinking and writing skills and helping others.

Writing a book is not easy, unless you enjoy writing (on a blog for example) like I do. You must have good reasons to write a book in order to successfully finish it and make it a hit.

---

[4]http://www.booksbythefoot.com

Here are the *good* reasons to write a book:

- You have something to share.

- You want to learn something.

- You want to check it off your bucket list.

Not-so-good reasons to write a book:

- To make tons of money and live *the author's lifestyle*—whatever that means (probably living on an island).

- To become famous: only in narrow circles of nerds and geeks (my pinnacle is shown in Figure 2-1).

- For prestige and reputation, or because it's trendy and everybody has a book: this is the worst reason to write a book. But without a doubt, having a book listed on a résumé is a good way to hack your way into a job.

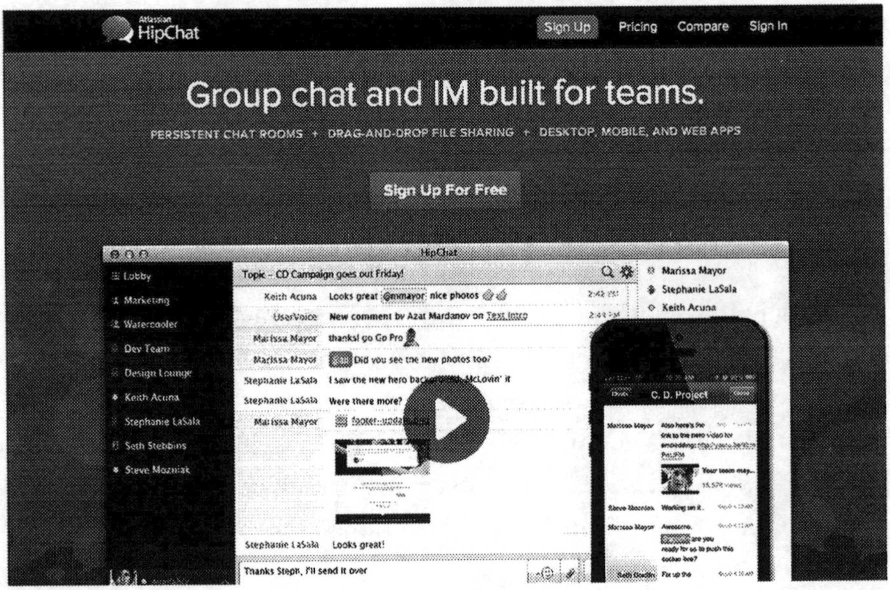

Figure 2-1. *Someone put my name on the demo video on HipChat's home page*

13

Why Write a Programming Book?

Why write programming books and not novels? Because anybody can write a novel, and the fiction market is super saturated. The demand is also higher (anyone who can read versus only people who program or want to start programming, as shown in Figure 2-2). However, because programming books help people to make more money and *they are not just entertainment,* they are priced two to three times higher, that is, $20-$50 per technical book vs. $3-$10 for a novel.

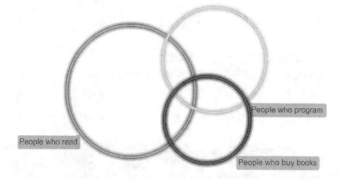

Figure 2-2.   *Venn diagram showing that not every programmer reads the books he/she buys while others enjoy free resources*

Traditional vs. Self-Publishing

There is definitely more money in self-publishing. The traditional publishing model is dying, or (depending on how you look at it) changing to adapt to the rapidly growing market.

Self-publishing is not new, but for years, self-publishing was frowned upon. Self-published books were mostly poor-quality books that couldn't make it through the editorial fence of traditional publishing. But this changed due to a number of things:

- Amazon's support of Kindle and self-publishers.

- Advent of better services and tools for writers (Leanpub, Scrivener).

- Established authors started self-publishing their new books, removing the stigma.

- New marketplaces for support staff: editors, designers, tech editors.

The main reason I went the self-publishing route with my first books is because I didn't think any publishers would offer me a deal easily. Therefore, I didn't want to waste time sending proposals. However, with my later books (*Practical Node.js* and *Pro Express.js* becoming a remake of *Express.js Guide*), I opted to partner with a publisher for the following reasons:

- Some 70-80% of revenue is still in print books (according to Guy Kawasaki's *APE: Author, Publisher, Entrepreneur* book)[5].

- I can reach more people. It's better to have an audience of thousands than hundreds because they can give you more feedback, and your ideas and practices can spread to more people (potentially bringing people better results and saving them time, which they otherwise would have spent scouring free blogs in vain).

- I can develop a stronger writing style and skills.

- I can establish my name and reputation (to boost the sale of other products and secure speaking gigs).

---

[5]http://apethebook.com

- Time-to-market is not an issue (the Node.js field is already quite saturated with good books, so time wasn't an issue as it was with *Express.js Guide*). In other words, self-publishing has shorter time-to-market and you can use the Lean Publishing approach.

- I can write about my experiences in future books (like this one!).

Typically, royalties can range from 6 to 10%, depending on the volume. This seems to be on par with the majority of the tech/programming publishing industry.

However, one publisher has a different model. In it, the company splits profits with authors, but my calculations showed that it ends up the same as ~10% of the listing price. It is, however, more confusing due to discrepancies in normal, promotional, and distribution pricing.

Remember, advances are not *free* money. They count toward your future sales. So if someone gets $3,000 in advance upon publication (a typical range for new authors is somewhere between $1,000 and $5,000), that means it will be *the last money that author will see in a long time.* This is because with 10% royalties on, let's say, a $29.99 listing price, it will take 1,000+ copies to break even and re-coup the advance. Sadly, 70% of technical books never sell more than 1,000 copies due to the narrow market and traditional publishers' poor marketing. Therefore, the advance is the only money the majority of traditionally published technical authors will ever see. Maybe that's the reason that more and more authors make their books available for free online in the hope of generating more buzz and attracting more attention.

Most traditional publishers do close to no marketing for your books.

As always, there are trade-offs and benefits. Traditional publishing gives a higher-quality product for beginner authors and the brand recognition, with the cons being lower royalties and less marketing flexibility.

There's no cookie-cutter answer here. Knowledge (such as reading this book) is a key component of success. While writing books is hard work, the rewards far outweigh any drawbacks. The benefits are there, but *only* if you're willing to put in the effort! In the following sections, I'll share how I produced and marketed my books. I hope my experiences help you on your own path to becoming a *successful* progwriter.

The Time Spent Writing

An average book consists of about 300-400 pages or 30,000-40,000 words. At a speed of 1,000 words per day, that's at least a month of full-time work (that's 20 days multiplied by 8 hours = 160 hours). This calculation brings us an average hourly rate of $18.75 ($3,000 divided by 160 hours). In most areas of the United States, that's below an average programmer's hourly rate.

ⓘ Info   As of this writing, the average rate for a software engineer in San Francisco / Silicon Valley is $50-$100 per hour.

However, if an author needs to perform extensive research, which is usually the case, and/or creates a few sample applications, the pace slows down, bringing the monetary benefit even lower. Sometimes I wonder if I can make more money by working at a coffee shop rather than writing in the coffee shop.

But there are outliers who make $50,000-$100,000 on their books. That's what you should aim for if you want to make big bucks in publishing (and I'll show you how to increase your chances).

For me, the realization that writing programming books generates serious side income came when I started making $300-$500 each month. I thought to myself: "Hey, if I can produce five or ten more books like this, it'll be a piece of cake to make a few grand per month!"

Before you get too excited about the process, let's dive deeper into what constitutes an author-publisher-entrepreneur process, using both self-publishing and traditional publishing.

The ProgWriter Creative Process

Yes, the *progwriter* term stems from programmer + writer, but in this day and age, it means a bit more. As Guy Kawasaki coined, a self-publisher is an author-publisher-entrepreneur, or as I call it, author, publisher, and marketer. So a typical progwriting process consists of:

1. Doing research

2. Picking a topic

3. Coming up with a rough outline

4. Writing and sending out proposals (an expanded outline with the author's bio, a writing sample, and the book summary)

5. Creating a landing page with a sign-up form or preorder option

6. Writing a manuscript

7. Technical editing

8. Content editing

9. Copy editing

10. Proofing

11. Publishing either with traditional publishers or by yourself; launching

12. Iterating, selling, and marketing

In lean publishing, an author might opt to release the book chapter by chapter, getting feedback and pivoting based on steps 6-11. For example, this is what a self-publishing process might look like:

1. Doing research

2. Picking a topic

3. Coming up with a rough outline

4. Creating a landing page with a sign-up form or preorder option

5. Writing a chapter

6. Technical editing, content editing, copy editing, and proofing

7. Publishing and selling the book/chapter

8. Repeating the previous steps as needed

9. Releasing the completed book

10. Iterating, selling, and marketing

On the other hand, there is less control with traditional publishing (but more help). You may

1. Research and pick a topic for the book.

2. Come up with a rough outline or several outlines.

3. Write and send out proposals to publishers.

4. Negotiate and sign a deal (yay!), and if you're good enough, get an advance payment.

5. Write a manuscript, and deliver it in one batch or chapter-by-chapter, which simply means that chapters can be in a different stage of the editorial process at the same time.

6. Undergo technical editing, content editing, copy editing, and proofing.

7. Initiate alpha sales.

8. Have the publisher release the completed book and collect royalties; if the sales are good, later, you can do a revised edition.

Step 4 is rather unpredictable and might take a few proposals to get a deal.

ⓘ **Info**   A proposal is an expanded outline with an author's bio, a writing sample, and the book's summary. The writing sample can be a chapter or two.

My personal observation is that lean publishing is better suited for established authors (or people with existing followings through blogs, newsletters, or social media) and for hot topics that serve a huge demand in the market. In other words, sell painkillers, not vitamins. *Sublime Productivity*[6] is a good example of such an approach.

In any case, make sure your book really shines! Don't permit any bugs or typos. I made this mistake with *Rapid Prototyping with JS* and got a lot of hate e-mails. Books are not like SaaS apps, which we might use quite often over the course of a week. Books are quite the opposite, because readers will, most of the time, pick up a book once only (or not at all), and if they don't like what they see in the beginning or TOC, readers rarely come back. Even if someone read a book, liked it, and found some minor issue, they rarely come back to its new revisions. Books don't produce as many feedback loops as software does. Also, the communication channel with

---

[6]http://bit.ly/1qx6uDy

books is not as clear as having a UserVoice[7] form on your SaaS application. I found an anecdotal support that forms work better than e-mail does, because people tend to perceive forms as less humane and less personal, and therefore are more likely to submit the feedback that way.

No matter what, make sure your book is well edited (steps 7-10). In this sense, books are like software: it's better to have fewer features with no bugs than lots of features with bugs. Again, I learned this the hard way when I released half-baked portions of *Rapid Prototyping with JS*[8]—typos distracted readers from my message.

For simplicity, we'll pack the aforementioned steps into three major milestones with traditional and self-publishing routes intertwining here and there:

1. *Writing*: The goal of having a manuscript with a market-validated idea

2. *Publishing*: The goal is to have consumer-ready files (usually PDF, Kindle/MOBI, IPAD/EPUB) and some sort of payment system in place

3. *Marketing*: The goal is to make the first sale and continue to improve the product

In Chapter 3 we'll look at the research phase of your future book project and a few other topics.

---

[7]https://www.uservoice.com
[8]http://rpjs.co

CHAPTER 3

Writing

Writing is fun, creative, and brings a lot of value to other people. But most people can't write a blog post, let alone a 30,000-word book. I think it's because writing is a habit, and it works just like a muscle that we need to train constantly.

In this chapter, I'll cover:

- *Researching the topic*: Before starting any writing, you need to validate a topic as market-viable.

- *Technical book categories*: Some examples.

- *Testing your topic*: Validating your concept.

- *Writing the manuscript*: The art of writing.

© Azat Mardan 2019
A. Mardan, *Write Your Way To Success*, https://doi.org/10.1007/978-1-4842-3970-4_3

- *Markdown for the win*: The productive way to write.

- *Health considerations*: Ergonomics, eating, fitness, and pacing yourself.

🐞**Exercise**   Go to this Amazon.com search result page[1], pick a book on writing exercises, and read reviews.

Researching the Topic

Let's say you have some ideas already. If you don't, then you have two options:

1. *New topic*: Pick a relatively new technology (e.g., React.js) that is hot right now and wait until it becomes—if it becomes—mainstream.

2. *Better book*: Pick a mainstream topic (e.g., JavaScript) that is already *hugely* popular, research the best sellers' flaws, address them, and make a better book.

It's a good idea to have a few topics in mind. Now, let's discuss the research to support or disprove your topics.

Needless to say, good writers are readers. In writing, your first move (after settling on some topics that are of the most interest to you) should be reading or at least skimming most of the best competitors' books. They are the best books on your topics, or related topics, if yours is too new.

Just go to Amazon.com and type the term, for example, "nodejs." On the first page, you'll see the best books according to ASE (Amazon Search Engine) related to this search term.

---

[1]http://amzn.to/1soNw3A

The next step is probably one of the most expensive phases in the writing process: buying the books. A few tips to help you avoid spending a fortune:

- Look at and use Tables of Contents for your research, for free.

- Use Kindle versions, because many Kindle books are less expensive than print books, and there are apps for virtually any device/platform/OS, so the *Kindle device itself is not necessary.*

- Go to the library and check out the books for free; however, this might not work with cutting-edge topics or small niche topics.

- Ask your supervisor to expense the books: I never received a rejection when asking for such things.

- Sign up for a Safari subscription—the Netflix of programming books.

⌕ Tip   To avoid spending too much time on research and reading, I highly recommend taking a speed reading class like Iris[2].

While you're on Amazon.com, browse through categories and open the books' first pages. Note their global rank. This is how popular the book is among other books on Amazon.com. Typically, the 100,000s and above is mediocre, the 10,000 to 100,000 range is good, and the first 10,000 is amazing! If you see that none of the top books in the category are in the first 10,000, that may mean the category and topic are not in such high demand.

---

[2]http://www.irisreading.com

Often books are placed in not-so-fitting Amazon.com categories, so be careful when comparing. This is done to push a book to be a best seller in a more obscure category rather than compete in a crowded but more fitting one. For example, *Pro Angular*[3] is #5,526 in Books and #4 in *Network Programming* but is not even listed in JavaScript, and it is a book on a JavaScript framework. Same with the longtime best seller in *XML Programming Node.js in Action*[4], which has very little to do with XML and a lot to do with JavaScript. Its rank is #10,487 in Books. In Chapter 5's "How to Improve Amazon Sales," I'll go into more detail about this.

Another step: Go to Google Trends[5] and search for your term. The trends should be going uphill, and not downhill. In an example comparing node.js and ruby on rails topics, Node.js crosses over Ruby on Rails' popularity (sorry!) in March of 2013, as shown in Figure 3-1.

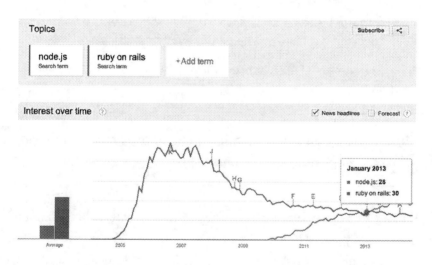

Figure 3-1. *Google Trends compares Node.js to Ruby on Rails*

---

[3]http://amzn.to/1plFFOC
[4]http://amzn.to/1reJtqe
[5]http://www.google.com/trends

Another example is if someone decides to write a book on a particular browser's JavaScript framework but can't decide what to pick. Among the top choices are React.js, Angular.js, Ember.js, and Backbone.js. A quick Google Trends query for the past 12 months, shown in Figure 3-2, puts Backbone at the top, with Angular trending up toward Backbone's ranking.

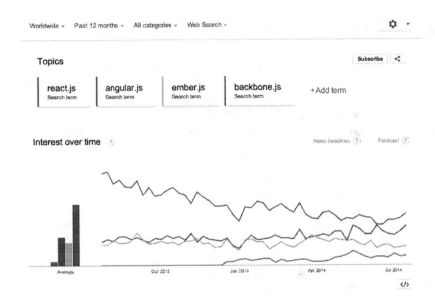

Figure 3-2. *Watch out Backbone.js! Angular is getting close*

Sign up for a newsletter on your topics to look for hot new frameworks that might need a supplement book. For example, for JavaScript Weekly[6] and Node Weekly[7] check out the newsletter by Peter Cooper.[8]

Join a local meetup or a virtual Facebook group, or a Google Plus community to stay on top of the trends. Hacker News, Geekli.st and similar sites are also good sources of hype.

---

[6]http://javascriptweekly.com
[7]http://nodeweekly.com
[8]http://bit.ly/2QmMjdB

🐞 **Exercise**   Pick a new hot tech framework or tool from Hacker News. Compare it to incumbents on Google search, Google Trends and Amazon.com.

Technical Book Categories

There are no set-in-stone categories for programming books, but most authors, readers, and publishers adhere to some conventions, which you can spot by certain keywords. For instance, "in action" means practical, "beginner" means no prior expertise required, and "expert" means it will be hard to comprehend without prior experience.

Here are some guidelines you can use to determine what type of book is good for your topic. This list can serve you when you come up with a title:

- *Introduction to ...* —quick start guide; audience: beginner; size: small, medium.

- *Concise book on ...* —gist/summary of the most important things; audience: beginner, intermediate; size: medium.

- *Cookbook/Recipes for ...* —a collection of practical solutions; audience: intermediate, expert; size: medium, large.

- *Definitive book on ...* —more like a reference or unofficial and expanded manual; audience: intermediate; size: medium, large.

- *Beginners' book on ...* —very approachable, tends to be larger than a basic introduction; audience: beginner; size: large.

- *Advanced book on ...* —meaty stuff for experienced readers that probably involves building some crazy ninja stuff; audience: expert; size: small.

The types might be mixed, for example, definitive guide with practical solutions.

Some concepts for technical books are

- *Language books*: The market is usually very saturated, so choose wisely.

- *Framework books*: An easy go-to niche because there are ten frameworks coming up every day, but the con is that frameworks die and become obsolete fast.

- *Tool books*: Usually a high-demand category, because of tools' lack of extensive documentation.

- *Service books*: A niche category, but as is the case with tool books, the lack of official docs creates a need.

- Blog to books.

- Programming-related books on careers, management, leadership, and methodologies.

A typical book length is about 300-400 pages, which consists of 10-20% illustrations, and about 30% code. This means that per 100 pages (8.5 x 11" with 11pt font size) there are about 10,000 words.

Testing Your Topics

The best way to test the topics of your choice is to write a few blog posts on them and share them on social media and web sites like

- *Hacker News*[9]: Minimalistic social news for hackers

- *Product Hunt*[10]: The place to discover your next favorite thing

- *Facebook groups*[11]: Various groups, such as JavaScript[12], which has 23,000 members

- Google groups[13], for example, Express.js[14]

- Google Plus[15] communities, for example, Programming[16], which has 126,000 members

- LinkedIn[17] groups

- Meetup.com[18] forums

To find a social media group/community, just log in to the web site and use search. Try not to solely ask or self-promote on these web sites. In other words, before asking for help contribute something first, such as useful information or answers to questions.

---

[9]http://news.ycombinator.com

[10]https://www.producthunt.com/

[11]http://facebook.com

[12]https://www.facebook.com/groups/JavaScript.Programming

[13]http://google.com/groups

[14]https://groups.google.com/forum/#!forum/express-js

[15]http://plus.google.com

[16]https://plus.google.com/communities/109728488971985783565

[17]http://linkedin.com

[18]http://meetup.com

The way I picked the Express.js topic is that a few posts on it brought 25+% of traffic to my blog. The decision to write a book on it was a no-brainer. However, I waited because I didn't want to be the first person to publish a book on the topic. In accordance with the technology adoption life cycle (shown in Figure 3-3), I wanted to capture a bigger market. Only after I saw that another Express.js/Node.js blogger released *a book on the topic* did I start the work on *Express.js Guide*.

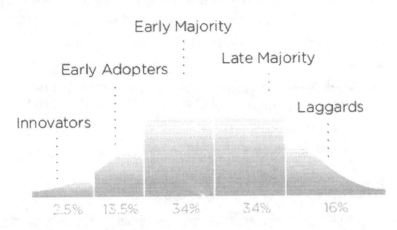

INNOVATION ADOPTION LIFE CYCLE

Figure 3-3. *Technology adoption life cycle*

An even better step would be to set up a landing page (buy an SEO-friendly domain for it!) with a sign-up form, or take it even further and start taking *pre-orders* with Gumroad[19] or Leanpub[20].

---

[19]http://gumroad.com
[20]http://leanpub.com

Once you've picked the topic, length, audience, and the title, and you've tested the topic to ensure that the demand is there, *get to writing*! No excuses!

Writing the Manuscript

As many prolific and successful modern authors have noted when talking about writing: *make it a habit.* I can't agree more. To me it's almost like *a muscle.* I started writing in a journal, then on my blog, and then books came naturally.

Some experts advise you to keep a pace of 500-1,000 words per day. But if you feel like you want to write more, don't let the word count stop you. Your writing doesn't have to be on your book's subject. Any type of writing can be useful in maintaining the practice and perfecting it. For example, you can write about food, or travel, as I do on azat.co/blog[21].

🔍 **Tip**   Turn off Skype, the sounds on your phone, and notifications; eliminate other distractions. However, some people need a certain level of distraction to keep them stimulated (like coffee shop noise or light background music), while others prefer complete silence like I do.

If it's close to November, sign up for National Novel Writing Month[22] (NaNoWriMo). It's a writing contest with the goal of having a 30,000-word manuscript by the end of November. The prize has no great value. The real reward is the writing that you'll produce and the discipline gained in doing so.

The discipline is important. It's extremely important for most of us who have to maintain a day job and moonlight writing books during free time.

---

[21]http://azat.co/blog
[22]http://nanowrimo.org

It's easy to get distracted by the errands of life. Try to find at least a half hour every day (morning, before my job worked the best for me), and write anything. If you can make it technical, that's even better. Your short posts can then be incorporated into the manuscript later, or serve as marketing material, which is covered in Chapter 5.

One last piece of advice: don't try to find a perfect day/night for writing. Just chip away at it anytime you have 5-10 minutes to spare. Of course long streaks are better because you can get into the writer's flow, which is a very similar feeling to the programmer's flow, when the sense of time is lost, focus and concentration are increased, and *awesomeness* is fired from under the fingertips. Tools and cloud services make writing anywhere easier. I've heard of someone who wrote his programming book on his smartphone while riding a train (saving to Dropbox[23] and publishing with Leanpub).

⚑ Exercise   Start writing a journal. Use Day One Journal[24], Evernote[25], or Google Docs[26]—whatever works for you. Keep writing every day for a week. Notice if writing becomes easier.

Markdown for the Win

Markdown is not a programming language in and of itself. The name is gimmicky, because *markup* means a language that defines metadata. The way Markdown works is similar to another widespread markup language—HTML—in which we have special symbols that define formatting and

---

[23]http://dropbox.com
[24]https://dayoneapp.com/
[25]https://www.evernote.com
[26]http://docs.google.com

styles in plain text files instead of relying on word processing software like MS Word, or Pages.

Why use Markdown vs. word processor vs. plain text? Have you ever caught yourself spending time adjusting styles, margins, and fonts instead of writing? Have you ever had your writer's flow interrupted by moving your hand away from the keyboard to find and manipulate a mouse to make some text bold? Plain text just by itself is not a solution either, especially for technical text that requires bullet points, emphasis, and code blocks. But what if we can define basic formatting with special symbols right in the text, right as we're typing? That is what Markdown is.

Here is a quick Markdown example:

```
1 *Italic* text and **bold** text.
```

Renders into:

Italic text and **bold** text.

Markdown was started by Daring Fireball[27] and quickly gained popularity among developers for documenting readme files (readme. md*.md is a markdown extension, but *.txt and any other extension works just fine because it's plain text!). GitHub spread markdown (with its own flavor[28]) *like a virus.* Then it conquered the hearts and minds of writers.

In this book, I've assembled a quick start guide: Markdown Cheat Sheet, which is located in Appendix A.

Health

I've heard of a person who almost ended up in the *hospital* trying to beat a book publishing deadline while juggling a full-time job and family. Don't overdo it. Be realistic when committing. A good rule of thumb from

---

[27]http://daringfireball.net/projects/markdown
[28]https://help.github.com/articles/github-flavored-markdown

software development is to *multiply the number of days/weeks by two,* or three if this is your first book, because everything usually takes at least twice as long as we expect it to[29].

When you write, use an ergonomic keyboard like Kinesis Freestyle2[30] (Figure 3-4) and an app like Time Out Free to avoid repetitive stress injury.

Figure 3-4. *Kinesis Freestyle2 allows for more natural separated-arm placement*

I personally maintain a primal/paleo lifestyle, which is akin to having superpowers[31].

🐾 **Exercise**   Try to do a 30-day sugar-, grain-, and gluten-free challenge[32]. See if your brain works better and you have more energy after lunch.

Fitness is as important as food—and we often come up with the best ideas while working out.

So now, once the first draft of the manuscript is ready, it's time to move on to publishing.

---

[29]http://en.wikipedia.org/wiki/Hofstadter's_law
[30]https://www.kinesis-ergo.com/shop/freestyle2-for-mac
[31]http://azat.co/blog/paleo-superpowers
[32]http://www.marksdailyapple.com/the-primal-blueprint-30-day-challenge

CHAPTER 4

Publishing

Instead of presenting an introduction, I would like to show you how easy it is to self-publish a book and start selling it. In fact, you can start *selling a book without even writing it* (it also helps to test the market demand).

These are the things you'll need to generate your first book:

1. E-mail account

2. Dropbox account

3. Text editor, for example, TextEdit, TextMate, Sublime Text for Mac OS X, or Notepad for Windows.

© Azat Mardan 2019
A. Mardan, *Write Your Way To Success*, https://doi.org/10.1007/978-1-4842-3970-4_4

Now, go to Leanpub[1] and register as an author, link your Dropbox account, and create the book by specifying some basic settings like

- Title (you can change it later)

- Landing page's slug (it's also changeable)

- Description for the landing page (optional for now)

Next, click the "Create Another Leanpub Book Now!" button (Figure 4-1) to create the book and wait until Leanpub generates and shares a Dropbox folder with you. This is your book's folder where you'll keep

- *Manuscript files*: Plain text files (*.txt) that have Markdown text

- *Book.txt*: A plain text file (*.txt) that sets the book's structure

- *Preview*: The EPUB, MOBI, and PDF files that are available only to you

- *Publish*: The EPUB, MOBI, and PDF files that are available to everybody who makes a purchase

---

[1]http://leanpub.com

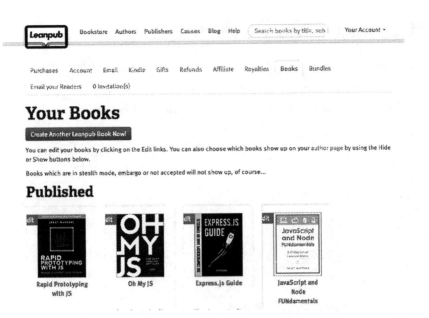

Figure 4-1. *Create Another Leanpub Book Now!*

So far everything is easy, right? Now, go to the manuscript folder, edit some boilerplate files, and then save them there. After that, go back to the Leanpub web site, and under your book's page, click the Preview button. Boom! Your first book is being generated. Very cool. But another great thing is that you're just one click away from starting to sell your book.

Everything sales-related can be done with Leanpub but, of course, you don't have to use Leanpub. Its policies are very friendly and allow authors to retain all the rights and sell anywhere!

Later in this book, I'll cover Gumroad as a selling platform and ways other than Leanpub to generate the book files in PDF and other digital formats.

Structuring the Book Properly

The most basic book consists of parts, chapters, and sections. The sections form a chapter and chapters form a part.

I like when the book has the following distinct fragments (in order):

1. Front matter

2. Main matter

3. Back matter

The front matter consists of:

1. Cover: Usually has a title, subtitle, author's name, publisher's name, and a tagline

2. Dedication: A phrase, such as, "To my son Oliver"

3. Foreword: A few paragraphs about the book from someone other than the author, typically someone with expertise and a good reputation in the field

4. Table of Contents: If it's an e-book, hyperlinks to the chapters will make the navigation better

5. Acknowledgments

6. Introduction

Typically, main matter contains all of your chapters, while the back matter consists of these components:

1. Outro

2. Further reading

3. Footnotes

4. Appendixes

Needless to say that many of these parts are optional, but if you want your self-published book to look more professional, your book should contain most of them.

Summarizing Chicago vs. AP Styles

There are many overall styles that can be applied when it comes to publishing your book. The most distinct are Chicago style[2] and Associated Press style[3]. The latter is from the world of journalism, while the former is larger and aimed at a broader audience of readers. Both have online and print versions for editorial guidance.

In general, AP style is more concise than Chicago, and prefers consistency and detailed attribution/citation. Here are some of the major differences between the styles:

- No spaces surrounding em dashes in Chicago style

- Oxford comma is a must in Chicago style

- *Coworker* in AP and *co-worker* in Chicago style (*Merriam-Webster*'s spelling)

- AP uses numerals (e.g., 3, 50), and Chicago prefers the spelling out of numbers below 100 (e.g., three, fifty)

- AP uses " ... " ellipsis while Chicago uses " . . . "

- Abbreviations: AP is more compact

If you self-publish, just pick one style and make sure your editor follows it. Keep all text consistent with this style.

---

[2]http://www.chicagomanualofstyle.org/home.html
[3]http://www.apstylebook.com

If you work with a traditional publisher, it will have its own style and will tell you what to use.

🔍 **Tip**   Here are some nice resources for deeper comparison between styles: Top 5 Tips to Edit and Write in Chicago or AP Style[4] and AP vs. Chicago[5].

Generally, Chicago is a default choice for technical literature. However, personally I've found that neither of the two aforementioned styles works best for me. That's why I have my own version of the style that I use.

My Style: Paragraphs, Lists, Asides

My style is a hybrid of several sources. For example, there are no spaces around em dashes, and my style forces the dictionary in my Kindle to treat two words as one (which results in no entries found). At the same time, I like to have the assurance of Oxford commas due to the importance of the technical text. More often than not, we just can't leave it open to the interpretation of a reader. *The clarity of the text is the author's top priority.*

To keep things simple, here is my style that I used in my six books:

- Use Oxford commas.

- Use numbered lists if the order matters, otherwise use bulleted lists.

- Introduce code with at least one sentence describing the meaning.

---

[4]http://www.proedit.com/top-5-tips-to-edit-and-write-in-chicago-or-ap-style
[5]http://www.apvschicago.com

- Try not to have more than five lines of code at once (without explaining what the code is doing).

- Name figures like this "Figure chapter name-figure name", for example, Figure 2-5.

- Introduce figures in text before they appear in the book, for example, "The result of this command is shown in Figure 2-5."

- Use inline code for function names, object/class names, and file names.

- Use asides for notes, tips, and warnings (see Appendix B: Tools and Services for asides).

- Use a monospaced font (and usually a smaller 9-10 pt font just because it looks better) for code blocks; inline code should also be monospaced, but it's better to keep the main text font size.

- Page numbers, footnotes for print versions (e-books don't need footnotes, because readers can just click on the hyperlinks), and internal links for navigation— if you use Leanpub or a traditional publisher, these things will be taken care of automatically; if you're not working with either, please do more research.

- Use "e.g.", "i.e.", "a.k.a.", " ... ", and "vs." with periods, commas, and spaces as shown.

- Indent every paragraph except the first paragraph after a chapter or section name.

So how can you apply formatting easily? You can use MS Word, Pages, or Markdown—my favorite choice, even when writing for a traditional publisher that requires MS Word.

Dealing with Source Code and Figures

I put the source code in the *public* GitHub repositories in addition to having most of the files in the books. For example, this is a repository for *Express.js Guide*[6]: `https://github.com/azat-co/expressjsguide`.

Normally, I list the code twice in the text of the book:

1. When I explain it line by line as we go along the chapters

2. At the end of the chapter/section to give the complete picture in case something is confusing

The code listings are started with the path and the file name, for example, oauth/index.js. This way it's easy to find where in the archive/repo this particular example is, and what file we are working on. I often include links to the GitHub repositories.

It's better to explicitly specify the language using GitHub style. For example, use triple backtick with the language name:

```
1 ```javascript
2 // code
3 ```
```

instead of just triple backticks without anything:

```
1 ```
2 // code
3 ```
```

As for the illustrations, all figures look better when they are numbered, for example, Figure 4-2 for the second illustration in the fourth chapter. Also, I reference/mention every figure in the text before introducing it.

---

[6]`http://expressjsguide.com`

Editing, Design, and Finding Help

There are a few types of editing, and they are best performed in this order:

1. Technical editing

2. Content editing

3. Copy editing

I prefer to have these edits happen in Markdown. I've tried many online Markdown editors, and Draft[7] is the most reliable so far, but even it can't handle texts over a few thousand words well. So, typically, I would use Markdown in an MS Word file with **Track Changes** on. This allows for effortless and errorless approval of edits. Then, I just paste the Markdown back into my Leanpub folder if I'm self-publishing.

⚲ **Tip**   Not all edits should be approved, because the editors might not know some technicalities of the text and therefore might suggest *the wrong edits*, which change the intended meaning.

In addition to the editing process previously described, I like to have an extra pass or two of the final print-ready PDF done by my assistant or another copy editor. People tend to miss typos if they are familiar with the text, so I always expect to have some errata.

upwork[8] is my sources for finding editors. I also use the help of a virtual assistant who does proofing and research and finds me the best designers and editors for a reasonable price.

---

[7]https://draftin.com

[8]https://upwork.com

99designs[9] is great for covers and logos. It's a crowdsourcing platform that will provide you with 30-100 designs for a fixed price. You choose the best in a few rounds of the contest. You can poll among your audience and friends. You can withdraw the contest and get your money back if there are no good concepts. All this happens in a span of a few days. I much prefer using 99designs over working with individual designers. Here's why: an individual designer (especially a designer you've never worked with) typically provides fewer concepts, takes longer to finish, and asks for more money.

---

❶ Info   "Don't judge a book by its cover."—People do judge books by their covers. It's sad but true. So either take advantage of it and create a good cover or get used to the fact that your books will be passed over for something else. My anecdotal sales data with *Rapid Prototyping with JS* and its covers proves it. The evolution of covers is shown in Figure 4-2.

Figure 4-2. *Evolution of the Rapid Prototyping with JS cover*

Unfortunately, working with a traditional publisher won't guarantee a good cover for your book unless the publisher uses a common style. While some of them are cool, the downside of a common style is that old-fashioned people, animals, fish, and insects have very little to do with technology. Sometimes it leads to something comically dismal.

---

[9]https://99designs.com

The lesson here is to retain creative control and be vigilant when working with traditional publishers.

As far as working with freelancers when self-publishing, here's my best advice: over-communicate your needs and requirements. *They won't be able to read your mind*—trust me on this. Write the job requirements once and store them in Evernote or Google Docs so you can easily reuse them later in case freelancers need to be replaced. For example, I've saved instructions for Markdown and Markdown apps because most editors don't know what it is.

Another tip that I started practicing just recently: have the first interview over video call, because it makes your contract more personal. Humans like to deal with other humans, and they will do a better job overall. After the initial interview, you can go back to chat, emails, and messages.

CHAPTER 5

Marketing

Most questions that aspiring technical authors ask me are about marketing. I think this is in part because marketing, selling, is considered by programmers to be some sort of voodoo magic. Most of us studied computer science and information technology—not business. But there is nothing magical about selling. In fact, we are all actively in sales throughout our lives. For example, during a job interview we sell our skills, on a date we sell our potential as a romantic partner, and at a job meeting we sell our ideas to colleagues.

© Azat Mardan 2019
A. Mardan, *Write Your Way To Success*, https://doi.org/10.1007/978-1-4842-3970-4_5

Marketing is easy when you think about the value that you bring to other people. Think about how much frustration, and how many sleepless hours, other developers can avoid by reading your books! If your product is good, this is exactly what will happen. Then it's just *natural* that you'll want to tell as many people as possible about your title. In this part, I'll cover some of the ways this message can be amplified:

- *Spread the word*: Let your target audience know about you

- *Have a platform*: Build it (i.e., a following) before creating a product

- *Marketplace vs. storefront*: Different ways to sell

- *Improve Amazon sales*: Tips and tricks to get to the top

- *Pricing*: How to price your book

- *Packaging and bundling*: How to expand your offerings

- *Up-selling and cross-selling*: Extra streams of revenue

- *Things to avoid (or do last)*: Things that didn't work for me as well as expected

Spread the Word

You are the main promoter and evangelist of your own books. Then come the readers. This is true even for traditional publishing. Use any opportunity to share how good your book is, that is, its key selling proposition:

- Meet-ups

- Conferences

- Co-workers

- Ex-colleagues and random people on LinkedIn who initiate conversations and want to chat with you

- E-mail signature

- Facebook, Twitter, Google Plus profiles, and links to a book on each

- Strangers in a Starbucks line—always have MOO[1] cards for them

- Public transport and airports, for example, wearing a laptop sticker or a T-shirt, and giving business cards to strangers

Always be selling! You never know where it might lead (maybe to paid guest blogging or a corporate bulk order of your books). My encounter in Starbucks with Startup Monthly[2] founder Yuri Rabinovich led to the Rapid Prototyping with JS training course and consequently to my first book.

Have a Platform

A platform—as in Michael Hyatt's platform[3], is the surest and the slowest path to success. In the simplest form, the platform is a blog. But it can also be an Instagram[4], YouTube[5], Twitter[6], or other following. The idea is to have an audience and a two-way communication. I prefer the platform and blog route for technical authors because

- It can develop writing style, habit, and skills gradually: Markdown, apps, the best time to write, and more.

---

[1]http://moo.com
[2]http://www.startupmonthly.org
[3]http://michaelhyatt.com/platform
[4]http://instagram.com
[5]https://www.youtube.com
[6]https://twitter.com

- It can judge demand for a certain topic, for example, What is hotter: React.js[7] or Anguar.js[8]?

- It can provide drafts and code examples for the book or even become a book, that is, blog to book.

- You can sell books much more easily, because your audience is already familiar with your works; for example, *Practical Node.js*[9] reached *#19,595* in Books on Amazon.com just *a few weeks* after its release (shown in Figure 5-1). The rank is for all books on Amazon.com, with millions of titles being sold there.

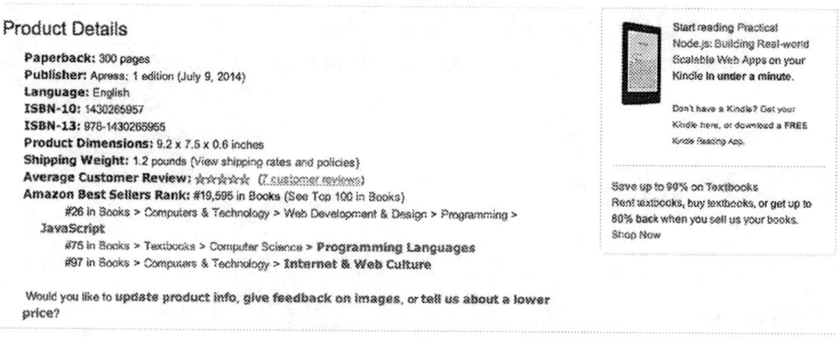

Product Details

Paperback: 300 pages
Publisher: Apress; 1 edition (July 9, 2014)
Language: English
ISBN-10: 1430265957
ISBN-13: 978-1430265955
Product Dimensions: 9.2 x 7.5 x 0.6 inches
Shipping Weight: 1.2 pounds (View shipping rates and policies)
Average Customer Review: ★★★★★ (7 customer reviews)
Amazon Best Sellers Rank: #19,595 in Books (See Top 100 in Books)
    #26 in Books > Computers & Technology > Web Development & Design > Programming > JavaScript
    #75 in Books > Textbooks > Computer Science > **Programming Languages**
    #97 in Books > Computers & Technology > **Internet & Web Culture**

Would you like to **update product info**, give feedback on images, or tell us about a lower price?

Start reading Practical Node.js: Building Real-world Scalable Web Apps on your Kindle in under a minute.

Don't have a Kindle? Get your Kindle here, or download a FREE Kindle Reading App.

Save up to 90% on Textbooks
Rent textbooks, buy textbooks, or get up to 80% back when you sell us your books.
Shop Now

Figure 5-1.   Practical Node.js reached #19,595 in Books on Amazon.com

So based on these points, I recommend starting your book with a blog. Of course there are exceptions[10], authors who created a following once their books became popular. But this is more an exception than the rule, because not validating your idea but testing it by writing 200-300 pages is time consuming. I would do it only if I absolutely wanted to write on some topic and didn't care about readership at all.

---

[7]http://facebook.github.io/react
[8]https://angularjs.org
[9]http://practicalnodebook.com
[10]http://thefoundation.com/podcast/episode46

In other words, for readers familiar with lean startup and lean manufacturing, with blog posts you can validate book ideas faster.

Marketplace vs. Storefront

I started with Leanpub because it was (and still is) an all-in-one solution:

- *Landing page to gather e-mails*: Minimal efforts to test an idea for the book.

- *Versatile publishing service*: No extra tools necessary—Markdown or HTML can be converted to PDF, EPUB, and MOBI.

- *Marketplace*: Its pages are SEO-friendly, you can bundle with other authors, and search can add extra exposure as well.

- Leanpub allows you to contact readers about updates or promotions.

Amazon.com is on the other end of the marketplace spectrum. It has more traffic and better discovery, if Amazon.com's algorithm picks your book, but no way to notify readers about updates or promotions.

It's fairly straightforward to build your own landing page, and hook up PayPal[11], Stripe[12], Plasso[13], SendOwl[14] or Gumroad[15]. The advantage is that you get customers' e-mails, better royalties, and more creative freedom.

---

[11]https://paypal.com
[12]https://stripe.com
[13]https://plasso.com
[14]https://sendowl.com
[15]https://gumroad.com

The disadvantage is that there is no additional exposure via marketplace search, and some readers trust unknown websites less than recognized brands such as Amazon.com (and its reviews).

My recommendation is to go to a storefront if you're generating traffic. My personal favorite is Gumroad, because it covers transfer fees and its interface is beautiful (e.g., Figure 5-2).

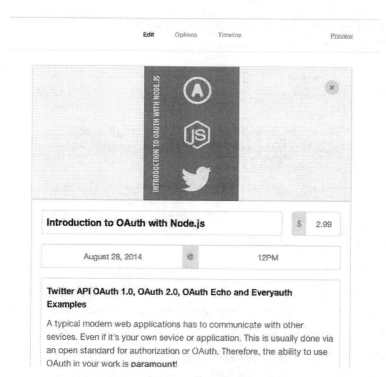

Figure 5-2. *Gumroad has low fees, and an intuitive and gorgeous interface*

Then, if you're optimizing for readership, make your book available *through all marketplaces* until you have a solid platform of thousands of followers. Some of the marketplaces where my books are sold are

- *Leanpub*[16]: Digital marketplace and publishing platform

- *Amazon.com's Kindle Direct Publishing*[17]: Digital marketplace

- *Google Play*[18]: Digital marketplace

- *iBooks*[19]: Digital marketplace

- *Lulu*[20]: Print on demand (POD) service provider and marketplace

- *CreateSpace*[21]: Print on demand (POD) service provider and marketplace

If you're optimizing for revenue and/or have a solid platform already, then *don't use marketplaces*: their interfaces are clunky, they don't provide customer e-mails, and royalties are dismal.

⚒ **Tip**   See *Appendix B*: Tools and Services for more e-commerce solutions.

---

[16]https://leanpub.com
[17]https://kdp.amazon.com
[18]https://play.google.com/books/publish
[19]http://www.apple.com/itunes/working-itunes/sell-content/books
[20]http://www.lulu.com
[21]https://www.createspace.com

Improve Amazon Sales

Amazon.com ranks each book based on a number of factors:

- Keywords in title and description

- Categories

- Reviews

- Sales

In other words, the more sales and positive reviews a book has, the higher in the Amazon.com search result it will be placed. *Survival of the fittest*. Think about the algorithm as a Google search algorithm.

So the title and subtitle are paramount—that's obvious. Don't choose them lightly. Spend some time and maybe even some Google AdWords money to test different titles.

In the description you can use a limited number of HTML tags to make formatting palatable:

- `<h2>`: Amazon-orange color heading

- `<ul>`: beginning of a list

- `<li>`: bullet point list item

- `<p>`: paragraph

Another important component is categories, as shown in Figure 5-3. The narrower the category, the easier it is for your book to become a #1 Best Seller. But don't try to trick the system by putting your book into a completely unrelated category. This might decrease exposure.

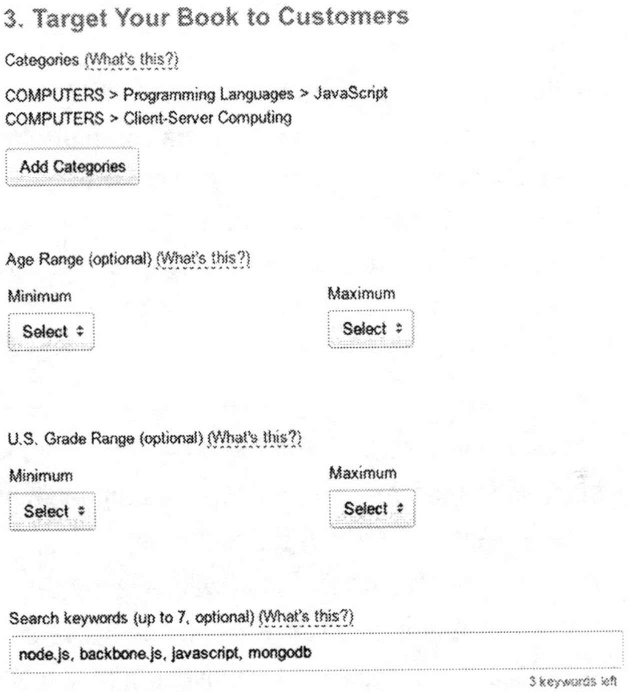

3. Target Your Book to Customers

Categories (What's this?)

COMPUTERS > Programming Languages > JavaScript
COMPUTERS > Client-Server Computing

Add Categories

Age Range (optional) (What's this?)

Minimum

Select ⇕

Maximum

Select ⇕

U.S. Grade Range (optional) (What's this?)

Minimum

Select ⇕

Maximum

Select ⇕

Search keywords (up to 7, optional) (What's this?)

node.js, backbone.js, javascript, mongodb

3 keywords left

Figure 5-3. *Kindle Direct Publishing form for categories and keywords*

Be sure to fill in the keywords in the KDP form. A bonus is if the keywords appear frequently in the title, subtitle, and description.

Amazon has a service called Author Central[22] where authors can create their *profiles*, so have one! Also, authors can link printed books to Kindle versions, monitor sales, and write additional descriptions for books.

Sadly, there is not much anyone can do with Amazon reviews. What's even worse is that some people will write negative reviews if your books start to gain momentum. Try to monitor bad reviews, and if a person just needs a clarification, *try to help.* This might help potential readers to vote for vs. against after they see that the issue the reviewer brought was moot or that the author (you) cares a lot and you're here to help.

---

[22]https://authorcentral.amazon.com

Pricing

Pricing is more of an art than a science. It all depends on the real and perceived values you bring to the table and on competitors. The competitor part is easy, because you can do a Google search or lookup on Amazon.com to find out what similar authors and their publishers—if it's a traditionally published book—are charging. It often varies from category to category; for example, Angular books are in the $40 range while JavaScript books are in the $5 range.

ℹ Info   Perceived value is how large the books are, including parameters such as format, font size, total page number, how good the cover is, how skilled and *famous* the author is, that is, credibility. The real value is how much time the book will save the developer or how hard the task it can help to solve. If a book can save seven days of work, that's at least a $2,800 return on investment, considering a rather low $50 per hour rate. In San Francisco, the rates for developers are in the $60-$80 per hour range as of this writing.

Self-published authors tend to charge *higher prices* ($50) mostly due to their small platform (and the effort that they've put in and the need to recoup). I personally *disagree* with such pricing, because they get way better royalties and usually their books are inferior to traditionally published ones. Most of my self-published books are priced two to four times *below* what a similar traditional book would cost.

Overall, the market for software and IT books is not as saturated as for fiction, therefore somewhere about $15-$40 is a good spot.

If you plan to sell on Amazon.com, the highest price that makes sense is $9.99, because for higher prices the marketplace will take your arm, leg, and unborn child (70% royalty). The way it works, you can choose between two modes of selling: 70% royalty, with a $2.99-$9.99 price window, or no price limitations, but only a 30% royalty. There's fine print as well—if you opt for a 70% royalty, Amazon can lower your $9.99 price at any time (let's say to $7.99) to fight with Barnes & Noble[23], or Google Play[24] marketplaces.

Therefore, for some authors it makes sense to sell only print books on Amazon.com.

As mentioned before, most authors opt to make their books free online (to get attention) and then charge for PDF/EPUB/MOBI if someone wants the convenience. In my humble opinion, this is a flawed strategy because most programing books are better to read on a laptop or desktop so you can run examples (not on Kindle or iPad). Nevertheless, there are a lot of success stories of authors open sourcing their books, so you might want to try it yourself.

Packaging and Bundling

Packaging is when (in addition to books) authors sell bonus materials such as

- Audiobooks

- Screencasts

- Action plans

- Interviews

- Source code (yes, some[25] coding books come *without* code!)

- Additional mini-books

- Multi-person/team licenses

---

[23]http://www.barnesandnoble.com
[24]https://play.google.com/store
[25]https://www.ng-book.com

- Case studies

- Templates

- Online access to e-books

Chris Guillebeau[26] and Nathan Barry[27] are famous for advocating packaging. I can see their perspective, but there needs to be enough value in higher-priced packages to justify the cost to buyers. My premium packaging for *Express.js Guide*[28] didn't do as well as I expected. I had online access, a mini-book, a cheat sheet, and a team license in the Professional package, as shown in Figure 5-4.

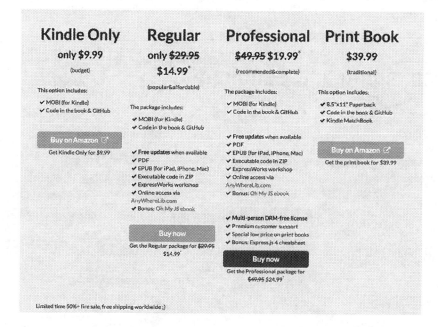

Figure 5-4. *Express.js Guide packages*

---

[26]http://chrisguillebeau.com

[27]http://nathanbarry.com

[28]http://expressjsguide.com

The weak sales of the premium Professional packages were partially offset by the psychological factor known as a decoy effect[29]. In other words, most visitors choose the middle Regular package instead of the cheapest Kindle package.

ⓘ Info   Decoy effect or decoy marketing[30] occurs when instead of two products, the seller offers three—with the third being inferior to the more expensive of the initial two, thus helping buyers to make a decision toward the most expensive of the initial two products. The decoy situation sells better compared to a situation with just the initial two products. Apple is a company known for practicing decoy marketing[31].

The print book is usually its own item because there are some people who love print books and others who would do anything to avoid buying/having them (like me!).

Bundling is another approach to increase sales. It worked well for my *Goodbye Express.js Guide*[32], shown in Figure 5-5, because it brought *a lot of value* to buyers (~75% off).

---

[29]http://en.wikipedia.org/wiki/Decoy_effect
[30]http://www.neurosciencemarketing.com/blog/articles/decoy-marketing.htm
[31]http://bit.ly/2QnZevU
[32]https://leanpub.com/b/goodbyeexpressjsguide

Figure 5-5. *Goodbye Express.js Guide rainmaking bundle*

Bundling also worked well when I partnered with other Leanpub authors for *Rapid Prototyping with JS*[33] (Figure 5-6), especially if the authors had been featured on the home page, because it brought extra traffic to my book, which I wouldn't have had otherwise.

---

[33]http://rpjs.com

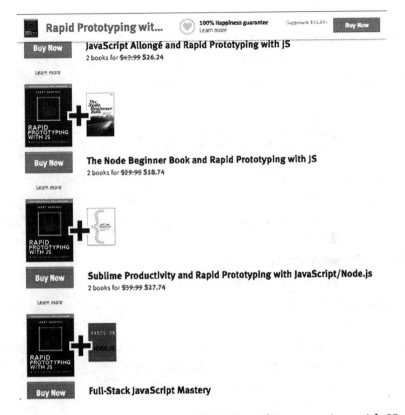

Figure 5-6. *Rapid Prototyping with JSRapid Prototyping with JS exposure-bringing bundles*

Mini-books like *Oh My JS*[34] and *JavaScript and Node FUNdamentals*[35] also work great to create value in bundles and as stand-alone marketing products when given away for free (not recommended) or close to free. For example, these mini-books with fewer than 200 pages together have 5,000 readers whom I can e-mail and cross-sell other products. Another benefit—if readers liked the mini-books, they have no fear buying more expensive products. Just make sure that the quality of any mini-books is

---

[34]https://leanpub.com/ohmyjs
[35]https://leanpub.com/jsfun

stellar (even better than the main books' quality), including the cover, and that they lack abundant errors. It's easy to fall into thinking that because it's a free book, you don't have to make it good. But this is your door to a new audience, and you should start with your best foot forward.

Up-Selling and Cross-Selling

Up-selling is offering an upgrade to the existing product (for example, going from a regular package to a premium one). Cross-selling, on the other hand, is a promotion for a different product or category—for example, purchasers of *Rapid Prototyping with JS* get 50% off of *Express.js Guide*.

They both are great things to have and use, because they bring in extra revenue that wouldn't be there otherwise. Another added benefit is targeting people who just made the purchase, so they have less fear buying other products.

Most of the platforms like Leanpub and Gumroad allow you to create coupons that you can paste into the products' thank-you or receipt messages.

Launch

Launch typically requires some sort of audience, maybe blog readers or an e-mail list. The idea is that the author prepares and educates buyers before the product is sold. This creates anticipation and momentum once the sale has started.

At minimum, you should do three posts/announcements:

1. Start of the book: to give the idea with a tentative Table of Contents (TOC) and description

2. Almost ready or midway ready: to remind the audience and potential buyer that the project is alive

3. Finished and ready to go soon: you're probably
taking care of some final finishing touches like
editing and covers, so it's safe to announce the date

Then you open the sale and collect money. You can also gather e-mails for preorders, alpha readers, and reviewers. Preorders come from people who make a decision now, but the delivery and payment will happen later. It's a great way to judge whether the pricing is right. Alpha readers are preorder buyers whom you sent copies to earlier in exchange for a promise of feedback. And reviewers are readers who typically get the book for free in exchange for the promise of a review. Google forms and Mailchimp work best for e-mail lists and announcements.

Gmail allows you to send up to 500 e-mails per day from one account. Just make sure to put the e-mail list addresses in BCC to protect their privacy.

It's easy to forget on what day or to what Facebook group or e-mail list you sent an update, so having a marketing plan and putting it on Google Calendar are great ideas.

Things to Avoid

I would recommend trying these things after you have everything else in place, because they didn't bring me the expected results:

- *Landing pages*: I would rather create a preorder page,
because interest from nonpaying users is not the same
as from paying ones (i.e., typically the interest from
paying users is less).

- *Facebook and Google ads*: Too expensive for a $15-$30
book.

- *A/B testing*: The traffic to most of my books' sites is too low (<100/day) to gather anything meaningful to justify the time spent setting the testing up.

- *Slow and super expensive editors and designers*: Unless you know that the book will be a success, it isn't worth the expense.

Support

One of the main benefits of self-publishing is faster and direct communication with readers. Make sure you have ways that readers can contact you listed in your book, such as

- E-mail

- Twitter account link

- Facebook account link

- Web site link

- GitHub repository link

GitHub Issues[36] are great at documenting existing bugs and typos, because GitHub provides visibility for others, unlike an e-mail. I encourage all my readers to go there first. Figure 5-7 shows fixed and closed typographical and programming errors.

---

[36]`https://guides.github.com/features/issues`

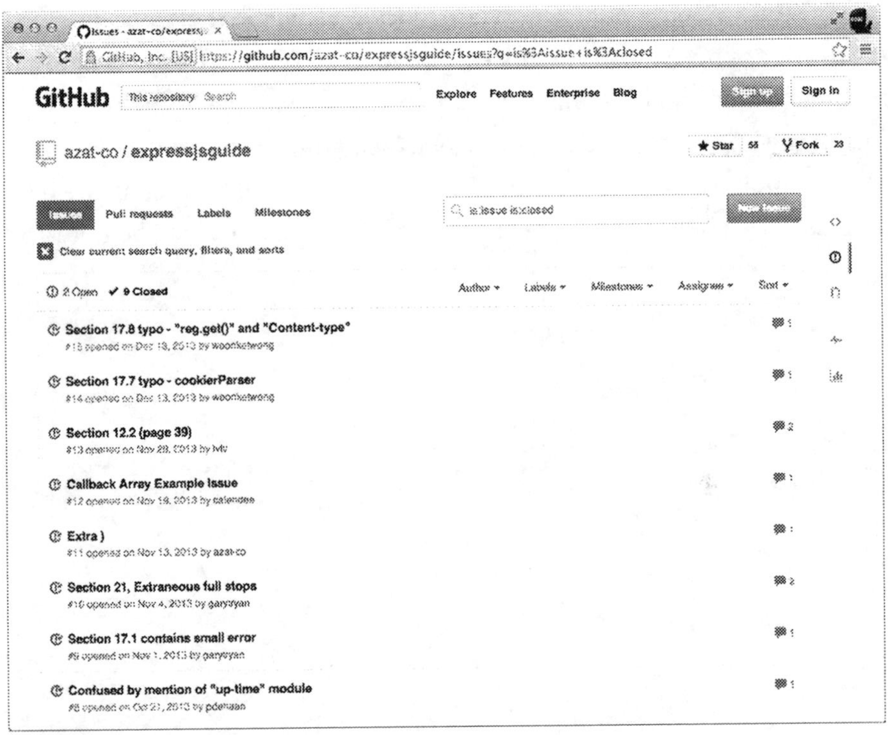

Figure 5-7. Using GitHub Issues for Express.js Guide errata

The shorter feedback cycle doesn't mean anyone should ship half-baked products full of bugs, typos, and the like. It means you can deliver less content, for example, a few first chapters only.

Once in a while, you might receive nasty feedback, hate mail, or a bad review, or experience trolling[37]. Try to learn, but don't take them seriously because in most cases these people either didn't read the book's description carefully and expected it to solve all their problems, or they are just upset with their lives in general. The best solution if there's nothing to learn—*ignore*. Never try to engage in a meaningful conversation because you are not likely to change their minds, but you will waste energy and time.

---

[37]http://en.wikipedia.org/wiki/Troll_(Internet)

It's funny to remember now: I had "a friend" tell me that nobody will buy my books because my English is not good, and just recently I got an e-mail in which a person was upset and tried to insult me because he bought the book at the full price, not at a discount, so I just deleted him from my mailing list. These types of customers only complain and are hard to please. It's a better ROI to focus your time and attention on the right people.

CHAPTER 6

Q & A and Random Advice

Some fellow software engineers started asking me questions about writing and publishing, which is the main reason behind the Write Your Way To Success book. Here are some of the best questions. You can use this part as TL;DR (too long; didn't read).

© Azat Mardan 2019
A. Mardan, *Write Your Way To Success*, https://doi.org/10.1007/978-1-4842-3970-4_6

Should I have a dedicated web site?

Yes, I would build a separate web site for any serious book (books at 200-300 pages, priced $5-$30), but not for mini-books or giveaway (marketing) books.

With a good title, meta tags, and SEO, your book's site can bring additional visitors. Also, it's good to have a canonical home for the book on the Internet, and readers are more likely to use the contact form than send an e-mail.

Just use a theme and GitHub pages (free!) for hosting—don't overcomplicate things.

Should I prepare a launch plan for my book?

It's probably a good idea, but between writing a book distraction free and finishing it, and having a launch plan (or other marketing) but never completing the book, I would choose the former.

How do I market to other developers (some of whom think everything should be free)?

You can try to educate people about why your product is better with free resources:

- Give a free sample of your book, which is typically the first few chapters

- Make the book free online, but charge for soft copies and print books (I don't like this approach).

However, I recommend focusing on developers who are used to seeing *value in paid resources*, because it's a better ROI on your time. Free riders will complain more. If they really want the book, they'll probably be able to torrent your book for free anyway.

What tools/programs should people use to write a technical book?

I use Byword[1] and Sublime Text 2[2] with Markdown, Marked[3] to check formatting, GitHub for backup and source code, and Leanpub for producing the official book. I tried Scrivener[4] and Ulysses III[5] but found them clunky, complicated, and hard to learn.

How do you go about editing and proofreading?

Typically I have at least two copy editors going through the text a few times. There will always be mistakes and typos. When I received proofs (final print-ready PDFs) from Apress, five editors total worked on the book. I sent it to my assistant, and she found more than 300 additional edits. So have someone look through both the manuscript and the final book. For the former, use MS Word with Track Changes, and for the latter PDF, use comments.

---

[1]http://bywordapp.com
[2]http://www.sublimetext.com
[3]http://marked2app.com
[4]http://www.literatureandlatte.com/scrivener.php
[5]http://www.ulyssesapp.com

I tried Draft and other Markdown online editing services, but MS Word still rocks, plus that's what most editors know and use.

Tips on topics or ideas to write about

Front-end/full-stack and JavaScript is the way web development is going, things like React.js, Angular, Vue, Elm, Elixir, and of course Node.js. On the DevOps side, Docker is popular. As far as tools, I would like to see a book on SourceTree.

How to structure the book

Keep things simple—parts, chapters, and sections, unless you want something more detailed.

How much to write each day

About 500-1,000 words seems to be the norm for people who have full-time jobs and families. This might take 30-60 minutes—not a big deal for most people.

Techniques on list building, beyond just blogging

Create giveaways, contests, newsletters, anything that might be of value to people to opt-in.

Should I create webinars?

Yes, webinars are great for connecting with your audience and making you stand out from the crowd of other progwriters! The cost is zero (just your time), and you get to communicate with readers on a more personal level. Webinars can be products in themselves, not just a marketing tool.

What do you use to publish books on Amazon?

I just log in to Kindle Direct Publishing, fill out the form, upload the MOBI file from Leanpub, and publish.

It's the same process with print books. I upload Leanpub print-ready interior files to Lulu and CreateSpace. The cover needs to be two-sided so a designer can calculate the gutter and bleed. Then, once complete, the file distributes to Amazon automatically.

CHAPTER 7

Successful ProgWriter Survey

Oren Ellenbogen

Oren Ellenbogen

An engineer who gets stuff done and enjoys delivering end-to-end magic. Curator of SoftwareLeadWeekly.com and author of LeadingSnowflakes.com.

What would you consider your most successful book?

Leading Snowflakes[1] (Figure 7-1).

Figure 7-1. *Leading Snowflakes*

How did you get into technology?

Starting at a young age, I enjoyed breaking things and figuring out how to get them to work again.

What were you doing when you decided to write your first book and how did it come about?

---

[1]http://leadingsnowflakes.com

I wanted to write a book about the subject since I mentored a few people in my team a few years back.

How did you come up with the idea for your first book?

I came up with the idea after giving a few talks (meetups) and getting great feedback on it.

What was the main reason behind writing your first book?

Helping others to scale their engineering teams.

How did you manage writing book(s) and other obligations such as work, family, and other side projects?

I'm planning to write a post about it—talk with me for details.

How long did it take to write the initial manuscript?

Five to six months.

What was your biggest surprise when writing your book(s)?

I could actually make good revenues from it. I'm an engineer, so I had to overcome that "sales is spam" state of mind and make sure the book had TONS of value in it, so I could feel comfortable selling it.

Did you use any external help to publish, such as traditional publishers, platforms, editors, or designers?

I used an editor + designer + freelancer to create PDF+MOBI+e-pub for me.

What has been the biggest mistake you've made when writing your book(s)?

Not building an e-mail list sooner (had ~500 on launch day).

How is your book(s) doing now, and what are your plans for the future?

It's doing well, I'm planning to do some guest-posting to promote it further. I'm working on an audio version and releasing a second edition later on this year (I hope).

What is the most important advice that you would give to a developer who wants to work on a technical/programming book?

Build an audience now. It doesn't have to be via writing blog posts. As I said, I've got a few writing hacks—talk with me for details.

What tools/services did you use to write/edit/publish?

Microsoft Word. Nothing special.

If you don't mind sharing, what was the net income from that book like?

$21,489 so far (4.5 months).

What attracts you to writing books?

It's scalable, unlike me giving talks.

Pedro Teixeira

Pedro Teixeira

Geek, programmer, freelancer, and entrepreneur. Author of some Node.js modules, the Node Tuts screencast show, the *Hands-on Node.js* e-book, and an overall fervent proclaimer of the Node.js creed. Wrote a book for Wiley on Node.js. Organizer of the Lisbon JavaScript Conference. Co-founder at Percent.io. Partner at YLD.

What would you consider your most successful book?

It was *Hands-on Node.js*—so far it has sold around 15,000 copies[2] (Figure 7-2).

---

[2]https://leanpub.com/hands-on-nodejs

Figure 7-2. *Hands-on Node.js*

How did you get into technology?

My father bought a Sinclair ZX Spectrum when I was ten years old. I started programming in Basic, then assembly.

What were you doing when you decided to write your first book and how did it come about?

I was having dinner with a friend.

How did you come up with the idea for your first book?

I had written some blog posts about Node.js, and a friend of mine suggested that I should write a book, since there were none out there at the time.

What was the main reason behind writing your first book?

Scratching my own itch: I thought there weren't enough resources about Node.js out there.

How did you manage writing book(s) and other obligations such as work, family, and other side projects?

I pulled long nights, sleep suffered, but I think I didn't sacrifice time with my family.

How long did it take to write the initial manuscript?

Took me around three months.

What was your biggest surprise when writing your book(s)?

How hard and time-intensive it was.

Did you use any external help to publish, such as traditional publishers, platforms, editors, or designers?

To begin with, nothing, then I turned to Leanpub.

What has been the biggest mistake you've made when writing your book(s)?

I wrote a book for a traditional publisher. I learned a lot, but the process is long and painful. The outcome was not worth it.

How is your book(s) doing now, and what are your plans for the future?

My initial book (`http://nodetuts.com`) is doing very well, especially when considering the bundle sales.

What is the most important advice that you would give to a developer who wants to work on a technical/programming book?

Don't do it for the money. Do it because a) you're passionate about the technology, and b) you're passionate about enabling other people.

What tools/services did you use to write/edit/publish?

I used Markdown, Sublime Text editor, and a set of handcrafted scripts to produce the various formats.

What attracts you to writing books?

Helping other people understand and become productive.

Maksim Surguy

Maksim Surguy

I consider myself a hacker/designer/entrepreneur. I like to make things work, either hardware or web-based. I've put my focus mostly on web development and in making tools that make it possible for others to achieve their goals, or be more efficient. If you want to know how something could be done, I am a great contact to have.

I was born and raised in Ukraine. I moved to the USA[3] in 2004 with my parents and my younger brother.

When I moved to the USA, I finished high school and then enrolled at Cal State University, going for a Bachelor's in computer science. I worked full time while studying at school for 6.5 years. I never got school loans, and paid for my education by myself. I graduated from CSUF in fall 2011 with a Bachelor's in computer science. While studying full time I worked at a school district as a computer technician.

In 2012-2013 I built over two dozen web sites in my spare time. Some of them you might have heard of:

- Bootsnipp.com[4]

- Laravel-tricks.com[5]

---

[3]http://maxoffsky.com/maxoffsky-blog/7-years-in-the-usa
[4]http://Bootsnipp.com
[5]http://Laravel-tricks.com

And many more.

Today, I live in the Seattle area. I work on my projects and am writing a book called *Integrating Front End Components with Web Applications*[6].

You can add me on LinkedIn[7] and Twitter[8].

What would you consider your most successful book?

Integrating Front End Components with Web Applications (Figure 7-3): `https://leanpub.com/frontend`

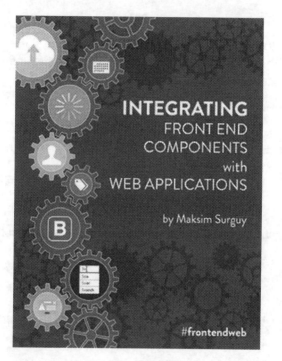

Figure 7-3. *Integrating Front End Components with Web Applications*

---

[6]`http://maxoffsky.com/frontend`
[7]`http://www.linkedin.com/pub/maksim-surguy/17/b93/a39`
[8]`http://twitter.com/msurguy`

How did you get into technology?

Here is a short list of things I excelled at in childhood and in my teen years:

At 9, I cut out some magnesium from a MIG fighter jet that was put on a kid's playground and used that magnesium to make small explosives and flashbangs. I would mix permanganate (a strong oxidizer) with magnesium shavings and pack them up in a paper envelope tightly. After setting that envelope on fire, I would run for safety and watch a super bright flash.

At 10, I won the regional Math Olympics in Moscow without even registering for it. I took the challenge just because I wanted to see how hard it was. The next day I found out I was a winner.

At 12, I replicated the Levitron—a magnetic toy that hovers in the air, defying gravity. I only found a small video of the toy in action and thought I would be able to make one. Taking a big circular magnet from a huge speaker and a small circular magnetic top, I was able to find the perfect balance of the weight of the top piece. At 13, I built my own micro FM—very fascinating!

At 14, I made my own LAN network using two wires, an LPT port, and an iron pipe that ran the central heating system in the apartment complex where we lived.

What were you doing when you decided to write your first book and how did it come about?

I was writing blog posts and decided to combine some of them into a book.

How did you come up with an idea for your first book?

I wanted to share what I have learned so far.

What was the main reason behind writing your first book?

Sharing my knowledge.

How did you manage writing book(s) and other obligations such as work, family, and other side projects?

I have quit my job to write my two books.

How long did it take to write the initial manuscript?

Two days a week for four months.

Did you use any external help to publish, such as traditional publishers, platforms, editors, or designers?

No.

What has been the biggest mistake you've made when writing your book(s)?

Not doing it earlier.

How is your book(s) doing now and what are your plans for the future?

This book (http://maxoffsky.com/frontend) is selling well. I'd like to publish it in a paperback version soon, if I reach $10,000 in sales.

What is the most important advice that you would give to a developer who wants to work on a technical/programming book?

Do it; do it now.

What tools/services did you use to write/edit/publish?

Atom editor, Leanpub.

If you don't mind sharing, what was the net income from that book like?

$5,000.

What attracts you to writing books?

Recognition, opportunities, making new friends.

Manuel Kiessling

Manuel Kiessling

Software architect, test-driven developer, Linux admin, Agilist, tech book author, father of two.

What would you consider your most successful book?

The Node Beginner Book[9] (Figure 7-4).

Figure 7-4. *The Node Beginner Book*

How did you get into technology?

I started to fiddle around with computers in my childhood and never stopped.

What were you doing when you decided to write your first book and how did it come about?

---

[9]https://leanpub.com/nodebeginner

I had a hard time getting started with Node.js development because all the info was there, but scattered around the Web. Out of frustration I started to collect what I learned, and that became the book.

How did you come up with the idea for your first book?

When I saw how much success the web page for *Node Beginner* had, I saw the chance to make that into a salable book.

What was the main reason behind writing your first book?

It really started just for fun.

How did you manage writing book(s) and other obligations such as work, family, and other side projects?

What worked extraordinarily well for me was to write a bit each morning and evening on the train to and from work. Also, the "never break the chain" principle by Seinfeld helps a lot.

How long did it take to write the initial manuscript?

About four months.

What was your biggest surprise when writing your book(s)?

How much money this can make.

Did you use any external help to publish, such as traditional publishers, platforms, editors, or designers?

Besides Leanpub, nothing.

How is your book(s) doing now and what are your plans for the future?

I'm currently working on the second book, available at `https://leanpub.com/nodecraftsman`.

What is the most important advice that you would give to a developer who wants to work on a technical/programming book?

Just do it. There is no reason not to.

What tools/services did you use to write/edit/publish?

Leanpub. It's the perfect solution, period.

If you don't mind sharing, what was the net income from that book like?

$40,000.

What attracts you to writing books?

It's great to share knowledge with other people, and it's nice that one can earn money with it.

CHAPTER 8

Outro

In ancient times, knowledge was often transferred verbally through oral history[1]. Then, the invention of Gutenberg's printing press[2] transformed the speed of delivery and spread of information. The accumulation and availability of expertise and skills led to an industrial revolution just a few centuries later. Many visionaries say that thanks to the Internet, we're in an information revolution. Companies are becoming smaller, many offices are now virtual, and micro-entrepreneurship is allowing more people to enjoy independence and better lifestyles.

---

[1] http://en.wikipedia.org/wiki/Oral_history
[2] http://en.wikipedia.org/wiki/Printing_press#Gutenberg.27s_press

© Azat Mardan 2019
A. Mardan, *Write Your Way To Success*, https://doi.org/10.1007/978-1-4842-3970-4_8

The best way to leverage your expertise or improve your skills in a certain area is to start sharing your knowledge with the rest of the world. And the written format is the best medium because it requires minimal investment and has the widest market.

Considering these factors, it's natural to see more informational products serving more niches. In this short book, I've shown you how in a span of two years I wrote several books, made a few of them stand out over the noisy crowd, and, most important, *learned a few things* along the way.

You should pursue your dreams. Don't postpone; start writing. Experiment, continue learning (conferences, courses, and other books), and as you improve, the work will become easier and more rewarding!

🐞 **Exercise**   Write, publish, and sell a book. Then Tweet me your story at @azatmardan.

APPENDIX A

Markdown Cheat Sheet

This is the absolutely bare minimum markdown cheat sheet I typically send to my new editors so that they don't edit out the markup symbols.

The headings are defined with pound signs (#) like this:

```
1 # - title
2 ## - heading 2
3 ### - heading 3
```

The links are defined with square braces and parentheses:

```
1 [title](url) - link
```

The images are defined similarly, like links, but with an exclamation point:

```
1 ![title](url) - image
```

The bold and italic text styles use asterisks:

```
1 *text* - italic
2 **text** - bold
```

The numbered list uses ones (1.), which automatically convert to the appropriate number:

```
1 1. - number list
```

© Azat Mardan 2019
A. Mardan, *Write Your Way To Success*, https://doi.org/10.1007/978-1-4842-3970-4

A bullet list uses asterisks with a space after each bullet point:

```
1 * - bullet list
```

The inline code uses back ticks:

```
1 text `code` text
```

And the code block (new line) uses Triple back ticks.

APPENDIX B

Tools and Services

I love to use simplistic tools like the Byword[1] and Marked[2] apps for Mac OS X. Byword by itself has basic conversion (e.g., Markdown to HTML), but I rarely use it. Instead, I preview Markdown in Marked, which has a lot of options and can support custom CSS (e.g., GitHub style[3]).

In addition to Dropbox's built-in backup, I also back up manuscripts into a private GitHub repository, while the books' source code is usually in the public repository.

Other writing apps to try:

- *iA Writer*[4]: A Markdown editor.

- *Mou*[5]: A Markdown editor and preview app.

- *Pandoc*[6]: A command-line tool for pretty much any conversion, for example, Markdown to MS Word; I highly recommend it, especially if you're writing for a traditional publisher.

---

[1]http://bywordapp.com
[2]http://markedapp.com
[3]https://gist.github.com/andyferra/2554919
[4]https://ia.net/writer
[5]http://mouapp.com
[6]http://johnmacfarlane.net/pandoc

© Azat Mardan 2019
A. Mardan, *Write Your Way To Success*, https://doi.org/10.1007/978-1-4842-3970-4

- *Ulysses III*[7]: A rather expensive and complex app. (I don't recommend it.)

- *Scrivener*[8]: The de-facto standard app for writers. (I don't recommend it.)

Services worth considering:

- *Gumroad*[9]: Has a painless and cheap storefront that I love to use

- *Lulu*[10]: Print-on-demand and a marketplace; the price per book for your own orders is higher than at CreateSpace (owned by Amazon), but the cut from other people's orders is higher

- *CreateSpace*[11]: Print-on-demand service (owned by Amazon.com)

- *Kindle Direct Publishing*[12]: Publishing platform for Amazon.com Kindle books

- *iBooks*[13]: Marketplace for Apple's iBooks

- *Draft*[14]: Version control and collaboration, or GitHub, for writing

- *Git Book*[15]: Publishing platform around Git

---

[7]http://www.ulyssesapp.com

[8]http://www.literatureandlatte.com

[9]http://gumroad.com

[10]http://lulu.com

[11]https://www.createspace.com

[12]https://kdp.amazon.com

[13]http://www.apple.com/itunes/working-itunes/sell-content/books

[14]https://draftin.com

[15]https://www.gitbook.com

- *Snippet*[16]: Publishing platform

- *KickoffLabs*[17]: Service for building landing pages

- *Unbounce*[18]: Service for building landing pages

- *Themeforest*[19]: Marketplace for themes and templates

- *Upwork*[20]: Freelancers

- *Freelancer*[21]: Freelancers

- *99designs*[22]: Crowdsourcing and contests for designs

- *Fiverr*[23]: Marketplace for cheap illustrations

- *Behance*[24]: Community and showcase of designers

- *VoiceBunny*[25]: Service for professional voiceovers

I rarely use online Markdown editors, but there are more and more services coming up that are worth considering:

- StackEdit[26]

- Markable[27]

---

[16]https://thesnippetapp.com
[17]http://kickofflabs.com
[18]http://unbounce.com
[19]http://themeforest.net
[20]http://odesk.com
[21]https://www.freelancer.com
[22]http://99designs.com
[23]http://fiverr.com
[24]https://www.behance.net
[25]http://voicebunny.com
[26]https://stackedit.io
[27]http://markable.in

- Dillinger[28]

- Draft[29]

Markdown editors for Windows:

- MarkdownPad[30]

- Texts[31]

The best writing hardware is the MacBook Air 13" (a MacBook Air 11" has a smaller screen and fewer hours of battery life). Why not Windows or iPad? In my humble opinion, they are less than ideal, although occasionally, let's say if you're stuck somewhere waiting—why not simply write on your smartphone?

---

[28]http://dillinger.io
[29]http://draftin.com
[30]http://markdownpad.com
[31]http://www.texts.io

Index

A

Advice, questions and
    editing and proofreading, 71–72
    launch plan, 70
    marketing to developers, 70
    norms for a day, 72
    publishing on Amazon, 73
    structuring the book, 72
    techniques on list building, 72
    tools/programs, 71
    topics/ideas to write, 72
    webinars, 73
    web site, 70
Amazon.com, 53–55
Amazon Search Engine (ASE), 24
Application programming
    interface (API), 5
Author central, 57

B

Behance, 95
Byword tool, 71, 93

C

CreateSpace, 55, 94
Cross-selling, 64

D

Decoy effect/decoy
    marketing, 61
99designs, 46, 95

E

Elance, 95
    Hands-on Node.js (Pedro
        Teixeira), 78–80
    Integrating Front End
        Components with Web
        Applications (Maksim
        Surguy), 81–84
    Leading Snowflakes (Oren
        Ellenbogen), 76–77
    Rapid Prototyping with
        JStraining, 3
    The Node Beginner Book
        (Manuel Kiessling), 85–87
Express.js Guide, 5, 7, 60

F

Facebook groups, 30
Fiverr, 95
Forrst, 30

© Azat Mardan 2019
A. Mardan, *Write Your Way To Success*, https://doi.org/10.1007/978-1-4842-3970-4

Printed in the United States
By Bookmasters